THE FANTASTIC FOREST

PATHFINDER EDITION

By Susan E. Goodman

CONTENTS

RUI VALE DE SOUSA/SHUTTERSTOCK.COM (TREES); © PHOTODISC (LEAF)

THE FANTASTIC FOREST

In the heart of the forest, you are surrounded by trees. Limbs tower above you. Leaves shade you from the sun. Birds fly from branch to branch. Larger animals, like you, walk across the forest floor. The forest is a fantastic place. It makes life on this planet possible.

What Is a

Oak Tree and Squirrel

An **OAK TREE** can be a home and a grocery store for a squirrel. **SQUIRRELS** help oaks when they bury acorns for future meals—and forget about them. A forgotten acorn becomes a planted seed.

Woodpeckers

WOODPECKERS drill into trees to find tasty bugs under the bark. Sometimes this helps rid the tree of harmful insects.

Bee

BEES buzz into flowers for nectar and leave coated with pollen. When they visit another flower, they leave some of the pollen behind. That helps the flowers make seeds.

Skunk Cabbage

SKUNK CABBAGE comes up in early spring so it can bloom before tree leaves grow and block the sun.

FOREST?

A forest is made up of far more than trees. It's a huge **community** bursting with bushes and vines as well as animals that creep, crawl, and fly. All of the living things in a community depend on each other. They also depend on many of the same things in their environment, such as water, air, and sunlight.

A Forest Community

Getting what you need in a forest can be tough. Some living things compete with each other for food. That means a plant or animal must battle other living things for something they need.

Some living things in the forest help each other. That's the case with bees and flowers. Bees need the sticky nectar inside flowers. As they crawl into flowers, the bees get covered with pollen. Then they carry the pollen to other plants. This helps the flowers make seeds. So the bees help the flowers and the flowers help the bees.

To see other ways that living things help each other, just look at the forest floor. Mushrooms and other fungi grow in the soil. Some mushrooms survive by breaking down dead wood. This improves the soil on the forest floor. Good soil means more plants grow and thrive in the forest.

Fungi

FUNGI, including mushrooms, break down dead wood and return some of the wood's nutrients to the soil.

Fox

FOXES usually dine on mice and other small animals. They also munch on berries for "dessert."

Earthworms

EARTHWORMS sometimes get breakfast in bed! They pull leaves into their underground burrows and eat them in safety.

What makes up a forest community

TREE-MENDOUS Gifts

Trees give us many special gifts, beginning with the very air we breathe. Air is a mixture of gases. These include **oxygen** and **carbon dioxide.** We need oxygen to live. The diagram at right shows how trees help renew oxygen in the air.

Forest Treasures

Oxygen isn't the only gift we get from trees. Trees help cool Earth by absorbing the sun's energy. They also act like huge pumps. They transport water up their complex root systems, through leaf surfaces, and into the air.

The list of gifts goes on and on. Trees provide homes for animals, and for us too when we use wood to build our houses. They provide food for many animals, including those of us who like pears or pecan pie. They give us beautiful forests to explore and the raw materials we need to make many products, such as paper and pencils.

Walk through your home. In every room, you'll find treasures from the forest.

PHOTOGRAPHS AT RIGHT:
BACKPACK: © PHOTODISC. CHEWING GUM: ALBUND/SHUTTERSTOCK.COM.
HAT WITH CORKS: © STOCKBYTE. PEAR: © PHOTODISC. WALNUTS:
© PHOTODISC. TOILET PAPER: © STOCKBYTE. SPONGES: © CORBIS IMAGES.
DOLLAR BILL: © BRAND X PICTURES. PENCILS: ©2012 CLEMENT
MOK/PICTUREQUEST/JUPITERIMAGES CORPORATION

HOW TREES HELP US BREATHE

1. Trees and other plants use light to make their own food. This process is called **photosynthesis**.

PHOTOSYNTHESIS

5. Then the cycle begins again as plants take in carbon dioxide during photosynthesis.

QUICK QUIZ Wood You Believe?

Here's an assortment of items ready to be packed in a camper's backpack. All of these items are made from trees. Some wood products are easy to spot. Other products made from tree chemicals and fibers may surprise you.

Sponges

The Oxygen-Carbon Dioxide Cycle

2. During photosynthesis, trees and other plants take in carbon dioxide and give off oxygen.

3. Oxygen is then released into the air.

OXYGEN

RESPIRATION

CARBON DIOXIDE

4. Animals, including people, breathe in oxygen. They breathe out carbon dioxide.

ILLUSTRATION BY STEPHEN R. WAGNER

© DIGITAL VISION

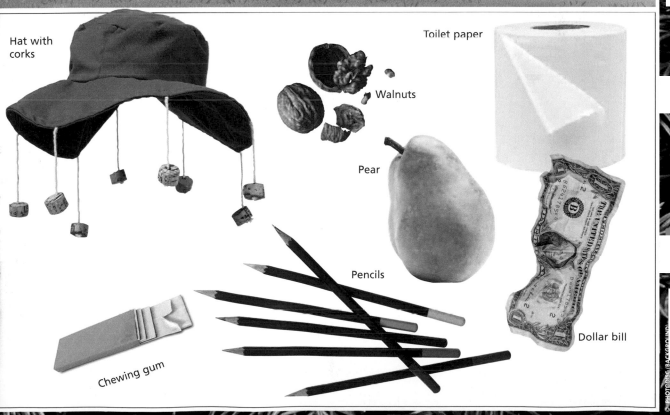

Hat with corks

Toilet paper

Walnuts

Pear

Pencils

Dollar bill

Chewing gum

© PHOTODISC (BACKGROUND)

FORESTS for Our Future

Nature supplies us with many useful things. These things are called **natural resources.** Natural resources include forests, water, land, air, minerals, and fuels.

There are two types of natural resources. Resources that we can replace (or that can replace themselves) are called renewable resources. Resources that are gone after we use them are called nonrenewable resources.

Old and New

Forests are renewable resources. We can plant more trees—and we do. But to make sure we have strong forests in our future, we must also sustain the forests we already have.

Scientists are helping. They are fighting diseases and insects that hurt trees. The U.S. government helps too. It keeps people from bringing plants that may carry harmful insects or diseases into the country.

We use more wood and paper today than we did 50 years ago, but we use less forestland to get it. How? We avoid waste by using the whole tree, right down to the sawdust. We have also found ways to make trees grow faster and produce more wood in less time.

TRY THIS!
Windowsill Forest

Potted lemon trees will thrive in a sunny indoor spot. Pot several trees and start your own future forest! Follow these steps for each tree.

1. Wash some lemon seeds with water.

2. Let them sit on a paper towel until their surface is totally dry.

3. Put pebbles in the bottom of a flowerpot. Add potting soil and moisten the dirt.

4. Plant three seeds about an inch deep. Cover with dirt and water.

5. Keep the dirt moist. In about two weeks, you should see some baby trees.

6. Let the best tree grow and snip off the others.

7. Water as needed.

8. Get ready to make lemonade—but not for three or four more years!

Fresh Lemonade 50¢

Wordwise

carbon dioxide: gas made up of carbon and oxygen

community: all living things in an area

natural resource: material on Earth that is necessary or useful to people

oxygen: gas needed by all living things

photosynthesis: process through which plants make food

Helping Our Forests

Modern forestry practices can help make wildlife habitats even better.

Careful harvesting allows the forests to grow back strong and more beautiful than before.

Streams and rivers need protection so all wildlife has good water.

Things made from trees make our lives better and our country's economy strong.

Taking care of our forests today means we'll have them to enjoy and use tomorrow.

Partial harvesting lets us use our trees for things we need—and grows a stronger forest at the same time.

Our forests give us a lot—oxygen, homes for wildlife, and trees that we can use to make the paper and wood products we need. We know that forests need special care to keep them beautiful—and useful too.

Forests need our help. We need to plant more trees than we harvest. We also need to use science to keep them healthy. We must all work hard to create forests that people can enjoy for generations to come.

FORESTS

It's time to go out on a limb and find out what you've learned about forests.

1 Describe a forest community.

2 How are forests important to the air we breathe?

3 What is the difference between renewable and nonrenewable resources?

4 Why do people today have more wood even though less land is used for growing trees?

5 Explain how forests help people and how people can help forests.

© PHOTODISC (ALL)